Women Survive ISIS

A long read by Judit Neurink

Original title: Vrouwen overleven ISIS

Published by Querido Fosfor, 2017

Cover design, based on art work by a Moslawi artist:

Annet Stirling

Translation: Pamela Williams

ISBN: 9781973504214

To all the Nadia's and Fatima's who suffered under ISIS but were able to pick up their lives and came out stronger

Other books by Judit Neurink in English

The Jewish Bride (novel, 2014)
The War of ISIS (non-fiction, 2015)
Slaves Wives and Brides (non-fiction, 2016)
Violence recycled (non-fiction, 2021)
The Good Terrorist (novel, 2022)
A Devil's Child (novel, 2023)

CONTENTS

1

A SEARCH

To live for three years under the control of an Islamic group like ISIS, also known as Islamic State or Daesh. Under a patriarchal system that defends values such as masculinity, fighting and honour. And that brands women as second-class citizens. What does this do to women?

That is the question that began to haunt me after my first interviews with people from Mosul who had managed to flee during the liberation, started by the Iraqi army at the end of 2016. As it had been nearly impossible for years to flee from Mosul, Iraq's second city with some 1.5 million residents was transformed into a large prison under the control of a vicious regime.

After ISIS captured Mosul in June of 2014, it continued seizing other Sunni cities in Iraq. Some 40 percent of the country fell under their control to become part of the Caliphate which was declared later that same month. Millions of people lost their Iraqi identities; from now on they were mere residents of the Islamic State and were ordered to abide by the rules based on the Sharia laws, and no longer on the Iraqi Constitution or the judicial system.

For the women, this had severe consequences. The Caliphate is based on the society in the time of the Prophet Mohammed –

fourteen centuries ago. Or at least, on the vision of that first caliphate in the minds of modern men. And that image is bad for women. They lose all their independence; they are only there for the husband and children. In fact, they are their husband's property, and that is why he is the only one who may see their face. And so, a piece of clothing that came into being in the desert where the Islam originated with the purpose of protecting hair and face from sand and sun, becomes mandatory in the 21st century. The niqaab or khimar, as it is usually called in Mosul, was a horror for many women. Moreover, as throughout the year, gloves and socks must also be worn, even during the peak of the hot summer.

The niqaab strips women from their identities in public life. Every woman looks basically the same, and for an outsider it is impossible to recognize someone who is covered according to the regulations. It strips women from the pleasure of displaying their best side or showing off a new haircut, beautiful jewelry, or a nice dress.

Although Mosul is a predominantly Sunni city and the niqaab is especially of piece of clothing for Sunnis, there were few women in the city who wore facial covering before ISIS - and some only when wearing a lot of makeup or when dressed up for a wedding.

Under ISIS the veil is mainly symbolic for the thick blanket of oppression covering women. With the exception of teachers and doctors, they are no longer allowed to work. In the streets, they are continually being scrutinized and punished for un-Islamic behaviour. Other women determine the punishments; and due to the facial covering, one cannot even know who they are. Fear makes its entry. Who is with ISIS and who is not, who can you still trust?

What does that do to women? How do they manage to survive and how has all of this scarred them? And what about the wives of the men who joined ISIS? Or for those who lost their sons to the propaganda of the group – or even support the group themselves?

Soon after the occupation started, I already spoke with

women who had managed to escape from the Caliphate, including many Yazidis who had been kidnapped from their province of Sinjar by ISIS to serve as sex slaves for its fighters. How traumatic their time with ISIS was, is clear. Their lives have been destroyed; they will always bear the scars from what ISIS did to them.

But is this also true for normal women, who were not a sex slave, but lived for three years in a large, women-unfriendly prison? Who did in fact follow the same Sunni version of the Islam as ISIS, but no longer recognized that faith in the way the group forced it upon them. Who disagreed with the way the society fell apart, in us, the faithful; and them: Shiites with the same Islamic faith, the Christians and Yazidis, the infidels?

Mosul is a special city to me, because a very dear friend in the Kurdish city of Erbil where I live originates there and still has family living in the city. Thanks to him, during the occupation I was able to get the latest news about the situation there. Through his sister Kifah, who had fled from the city but like a spider in a web still maintained contact with the family by phone – even when this was forbidden and could cost you your life.

Talking to Kifah connected me to the entire family. I mourned with them when one of the sons, who were police officers, was executed by ISIS. I shared the horror as one of the sisters was used as a human shield and when the family house was bombed. And I always wanted to know more. About emotions, traumas and especially about survival.

After the liberation of parts of Mosul, I am finally able to visit them myself and ask them, and later also other women, what the occupation has done to them. Are there permanent consequences? And are they only negative?

+++

Is it possible that something so negative can also have positive results? The Kurdish sociologist Chnar Abdullah told me in an interview that with the tragedy of the Yazidis – the more than six thousand women and children who were kidnapped and the thousands of men murdered by ISIS – she was still able to see a silver lining. She experienced problems after I had published that, because for the Kurds this was like swearing in church to suggest that genocide, such as they had experienced in the eighties under the Iraqi dictator Saddam Hussein, could also have any positive effect.

Abdullah concluded that the closed society of the Yazidis opened up under the pressure of what had happened to their women. What normally would be a long process, now happened at a greatly accelerated rate. 'The war has sad consequences, but we will also see positivity in the future. Society will no longer be the same. It will be more open, the level of education will be raised, the role of women will increase, and the power of the religion will diminish.'

The changes actually already began with the return of the raped women. Thanks to a decision by the religious leadership of the Yazidis, they were cleansed of any blame. Abdullah viewed this as being defining for the reaction of the group and the changes it is experiencing. 'Previously, a girl who had fallen in love with someone from another faith would have been murdered! But now they view the women as victims and try not to kill them. That means that the society is trying to break with old values.'

The sociologist saw that women who had returned, emancipated. Like Nadia Murad, a young Yazidi woman who told the story of her kidnapping, repeated selling and rape, and by doing so gained global attention for the fate of the Yazidis under the control of ISIS. 'If these crimes had not been committed, who would have known her? We had perhaps never even heard her name. Now we not only know her, but many other Nadias as well.'

Women enter the spotlight. 'How many Yazidi men do you see talking publicly about the story? It is especially women like Nadia. Women who were victims become leaders who tell the story of what has happened to the Yazidis. They have become a symbol for their society.'

This transition will not be an easy one, Abdullah warned. 'There will be problems. Conflicts between young and old, women and men. Because those do not want to lose their power. It can be a hard and dangerous confrontation. Men can attempt to bring the women under control by using violence. But there has already been a change. The clock can no longer be turned back.'

Abdullah emphasized that the negative effect of what ISIS did to women cannot be denied. 'Not only will this generation be traumatized, but also the next. What happened under ISIS will haunt these women for the rest of their lives.'

But from the adage 'what doesn't kill you makes you stronger,' the horrific experiences under ISIS could in the long term also lead to growth and development. I wondered how much of this would become evident following the liberation. And at the same time, I reminded myself of a story that Chnar Abdullah also told me: about the widows of the thousands of men from the Barzani-tribe that Saddam Hussein murdered in the eighties. The women, villagers from a conservative society, all were left behind with their children, after their men were taken away to die in the desert in South-Iraq. 'They had no choice; they were forced into the role of both father and mother and had to raise their children on their own. Their role changed.'

Many of their sons now declare their pride for their strong mothers, Abdullah told me. The women searched for work, a taboo up till then, and evolved to be able to handle their heavy task. It changed their lives. But did it also have consequences for society? Because although that pride extended far beyond the family unit, they did not become a shining example for other women and therefore no emancipation process got underway. I do not know of any academic research done into the matter, probably because there was little to discover.

The situation of the women in Mosul can perhaps best be compared to that of the Barzani-women, before that of the Yazidis. ISIS treated all women badly, but with the Yazidis that was to a superlative degree. Does that play a role when it comes to the degree of trauma, and could it be that only the deepest depths of humiliation lead to change? Or not? Will the women of Mosul also come out stronger after the horrors they have survived?

2

THE LIVES OF WOMEN UNDER ISIS

As the first neighbourhoods of East-Mosul are liberated, some of my friend's family members from Mosul manage to join his younger sister Kifah (47) in Erbil. I meet her sisters Alya (68) and Afaf (44), and while Alya's grandchildren run in and out with her sisters' children, Kifah serves sweet tea and coffee. While the muted television in the corner continues to repeat the same news, I ask about their stories.

Fear is the common thread that binds each and every story. I discover that with everything that I know about the rules and habits of ISIS, these women still manage to surprise me. And once again I am impressed about the resilience and creativity with which people have managed to survive; how women were able to keep everything together when poverty made its entrance after the disappearance of any work and income. But also, how behind the closed gates women tried to hang on to normality by still dressing up and using make-up. And how hairdressers and beauty parlours kept working in secret, although now mostly at their customers' homes.

I find that the notion that women's lives in the Caliphate took place mainly outside of the public domain, is far too simple. Certainly, women were only permitted to go outside when accompanied by a male family member and while covered from head to toe in black cloth. Even taxi drivers refused to take women who were alone. Many women preferred to remain at home, rather than be confronted by the morality police, the so-called hisba, or punished by the women's branch of it, simply because her socks are too transparent or her shoes not black, or because her black caftan has embroidery work, and the compulsory three layers of fabric fails to hide her face. Which limits her field of vision so much that women feel uncertain when walking outside, and often stumble and fall.

The stories about the morality police's reign of terror have been revealed even before the liberation, but I found their alleged use of a metal instrument known as 'the biter' hard to believe. In Kifah's sunny living room, the horror stories seem unstoppable. Like the one about the 11-year-old girl who used the water hose to clean the pavement outside of her parents' house. 'The hisba knocked on the gate and asked to see the woman who had just been outside cleaning the stoop,' Neno, Afaf's adult daughter tells me. 'The father then said; she is only a child. But she had to be punished for being out on her own, and was given the choice to be beaten with a whip, or punished using the biter. The girl chose the latter, and died from shock when she experienced what it was. Her mother went mad, and ran screaming in the street that Daesh had murdered her child.'

The biter is exactly what the name means: it takes a bite of your flesh, and usually the Syrian women who carried out the punishments chose to bite in the breast, which resulted in serious injuries. There are numerous reports of women bleeding to death or dying from their wounds.

ISIS maintained a policy in which people were unsure of what they could expect, which caused great fear and ensured that no one trusted anyone anymore. Everyone could betray you, as an eighteen-year-old girl discovered after having complained about ISIS in the garden to the woman next door. 'Someone heard it, and the same evening the hisba came and took her away,' Alya explained. 'Her father wanted to go along but was not allowed. The next day he was invited to come and get her corpse from the morgue.'

And yet another such story that shows the level of cruelty the citizens were faced with. Alya: 'A mother was so angry with her child, that she swore to God that she would kill it. A member of the hisba outside of the gate heard this. He said: "Because you have sworn this, you must now kill her." When she could not do it, he did.'

+++

How much fear can a person handle? It doesn't really surprise me to hear that everyday life also continued. We know this from stories during WWII too. Marriages were still taking place, and that had to be celebrated, despite efforts by ISIS to discourage this. The DJ was banned because music was forbidden. And if there was any singing during the wedding ceremony, the groom would be taken away and given a hundred lashes by whip.

Alya remembers a wedding within the family, that was held in a house. 'One of the young women had been caught wearing high heels underneath the khimar. She hid herself. Daesh demanded that she be brought to them, otherwise they would take away the groom. We refused, and then when we left, we bound plastic bags around our feet instead of our shoes with high heels to keep from being caught.'

Shopping, for many women in Iraq a necessity of life, becomes less attractive when you always have to be accompanied by your husband or son, and run the risk of being caught for something that's wrong with your clothing. And how can you do the shopping, if contact between men and women is limited? Afaf tells me, and later I hear the same thing from a shopkeeper in a market in East-Mosul, that the seller would sit in front of his shop, while his wife and daughters would handle the sales inside. 'The plastic bag with clothes had to be dark, and not transparent,' Afaf sniffles.

These are relatively minor problems, in a city where even smoking a cigarette is a crime and where people are being executed on a weekly basis. 'Our family had the least of the problems,' Alya says, putting things in perspective.

Her younger sister has just talked about their fears during the liberation. They had yearned for the arrival of the Iraqi army, which by the end of 2016 had liberated a number of neighbourhoods in East-Mosul. But ISIS sent its fighters into the neighbourhoods to attack the army. In the fire fights, hundreds of civilians were killed. 'On the night of the liberation, we saw Daesh enter the home of the neighbours with two wounded. My brother-in-law went to check it out and they said that he was to remain inside and be quiet. We could hear them firing rounds of mortars from the roof. We were terrified that the planes would come and bomb the house. The entire family stayed hidden underneath the stairs for a day.'

That the claim Alya made about her family being lucky is not completely true, I already know before I visit another part of the family that remained. Her brother Nasser (58) and his three children have recently arrived in the liberated East of Mosul from the west side. There, the old family home had been heavily damaged after the homes next door were bombed. Interior walls had collapsed but they managed to escape with only minor injuries. Nasser mourned the loss of his car, which he used to transport goods for a fee and that had been set on fire by ISIS with dozens other cars, so that the smoke would block the view for the bomber planes above.

His daughters Mays (21) and Marwa (22) tell me how shocked they were when on their way to East-Mosul, they saw the corpses of women and children lying about. ISIS had shot and killed them simply for trying to escape. During the last months of the liberation, hundreds of women and children were shot and killed without mercy. The Americans used phosphoric bombs to create smoke screens and protect the troops trying to save the wounded civilians.

But when the young women talk about their lives under ISIS, it's mainly about the boredom, because they could no longer attend university. Mays was studying English, and Marwa was going to art college. Shortly after the occupation, English was banned for being the language of the enemy, but when ISIS realized that many of its fighters spoke it, that decision was revoked. For Marwa, the situation was the most threatening of the two sisters, because ISIS had forbidden all art that did not serve God. Out of fear she burned years of her work, even though she kept a few photos on her cell phone. Aunt Nidal (61), who had fled earlier and with whom they are now living, presents a painting that she had taken when she fled. Some of Marwa's earlier work; a forest scene with lots of green.

The women talk about the joy they felt when after the liberation the Iraqi soldiers asked them to take off their niqaab; a video is circulating of the party in the street with the army. 'I have banned black,' Mays says. But Mosul still remains a conservative city and Mays is wearing a dark-blue headscarf loosely over her dark hair, and so does Marwa. A cousin appears wearing tight jeans, but the sisters stick with long skirts and light-coloured blouses.

Clothing – for us it is so normal just to wear whatever you want. To make yourself look beautiful, or just enjoy walking around in a new dress. For three years, only being allowed outside wearing black while you hate it, leads to extreme reactions. Escape routes used by displaced persons to get out of Mosul are littered with black cloth. And from early 2017, the same goes for Raqqa. Women cast off the hated niqaab, as their first deed of liberation.

+++

Just how important it is after ISIS, to dress with care, I notice when I meet Esma (27) and her daughters Nama and Sidra. I meet them at Kifah's house, who has introduced us because Esma has so many stories. Indeed, she is an avid storyteller. When she says that even twelve-year-old Sidra was forced to wear a niqaab, and nine-year-old Nama long skirts, Sidra makes a face. 'They cried when they had to put them on,' her mother says. Sidra: 'I didn't look nice.'

In the three years under the control of ISIS, there was no room for vanity. The most important thing was to try not to draw attention to yourself and run the risk of a painful punishment. 'If we went outside, my husband always checked to see if we had everything on. Socks, gloves... I was always the first one to take off my khimar. That felt like freedom,' Esma tells me. She has traded in the black for a scarf, blouse and a long skirt in various shades of brown, while this time Kifah is wearing long black pants and a red sweater – I've never seen her dressed this modern before. The daughters wear knitted and crocheted dresses in bright colours – the result of their mother's attempt to still have some earnings while under the control of ISIS.

In a city where the majority of the residents were reliant on a governmental income, money became scarce when the Iraqi government stopped the payment of salaries in 2015. Those with a family member receiving a government pension were lucky, as that did continue, and this allowed multiple families to survive. Others, like my adopted family in Mosul, received money from family members outside of the Caliphate. Esma searched for a source of income when her husband, who was a rice trader, received a large fine, and found the answer in organising a knitting course.

She rented a former pool hall – because playing pool was now also forbidden – and had no trouble in getting women interested. 'I gave six courses, each with fifteen women, including doctors and architects. They were tired of sitting at home and this was a distraction.' She shows me pictures of a graduation party, in the same space, with colourfully dressed women wearing heavy make-up.

But within no time, the morality police began to harass her students. 'They followed them home after the classes, knocked on the door and asked to see them.' The hisba could often be found hanging around the building, and it was their greatest hobby to try and get a glimpse of the training space, 'to see who was wearing mascara of eyeliner, because we also gave advice about cosmetics.'

Her cousin became the victim of the overzealous attention of the morality police. 'She had forgotten the second layer of the khimar and was wearing mascara. She was summoned to the hisba office with her brother. He discovered a new instruction there: if a woman with mental health issues was found without a khimar or with makeup, she was not to be punished. He told the hisba: "She is crazy; we cannot keep her under control." They let her go.'

The hisba was feared amongst the women. 'If we heard the hisba coming, then that meant death in the neighbourhood,' Esma says. It sounds melodramatic, but then she talks about how one of her students left the class and noticed that an officer was watching, while she realized that her yellow was visible under her black clothes. 'She desperately tried to cover herself. Her husband was there waiting in the car, and she got inside and made herself as small as possible to remain unseen. From fear, she went into shock, was hospitalized for three days and was left with a poorly functioning liver.'

The hisba was everywhere, and the stories are feeding my suspicion that many of the officers were using their job for the sole purpose of being able to watch women. In a society where men and women are separated from one another, it must have given them great pleasure.

Some hisba officers were bullies, or they used their jobs to enrich themselves. Esma's husband took their daughter to the park during the Eid al-Adha, as it was nice weather and many people wanted to go outside. 'The hisba was walking around and standing by the entrance. If they saw a woman with a khimar that did not have three layers of fabric, then she was given a fine of 50.000 dinar.'

Thirty-seven euro ($43) is a huge amount in a society where there is nearly no money left at all. Esma recounts a verbal exchange with the hisba in the park, after a woman had lifted her niqaab just to be able to eat. 'Her husband said: "None of you are men, you are all weaklings." That was a big insult, and the hisba arrested all of men.'

ISIS changed the lives of women in a drastic way. They were no longer allowed to work and were in fact condemned to staying at home. 'They said that the woman is the queen of her home,' Esma says with a sneer, since she was no longer allowed to attend her studies at the university. She always enjoyed walking there, and now that too was no longer possible. For three years she hardly ever went to the market. 'Except to buy material for the classes, and then I came back right away.' Because there were women from the hisba walking around there, 'with a green band around their heads with on it the declaration of faith. They had a weapon and a biter, and one of them bit me in the hand and arm just because I started a discussion with her.'

After Esma had given six classes, ISIS put an end to it. 'Perhaps they thought I was trying to turn the women against them. They opposed all forms of gatherings,' she says. I think that she is right. The leaders of ISIS knew that many women felt strongly about the instructions that changed their lives. They were very watchful to prevent any organized protest from taking place. Individual women tell me about arguments with the hisba that they often managed to win by causing a commotion that left the men at odds about what to do. That changed when ISIS decided that a woman who voiced opposition was to be handed over to the special women's brigade. That did not allow itself to be manipulated and took those women causing problems away to be punished.

Esma tells me how the hisba once came into her classroom, and that the discovery of a sheet of paper about applying make-up was reason enough to take her along for questioning. 'I told them that I was teaching the women to knit and sew, and that there were also Daesh women participating.'

It was the first time that she let it slip that women who were involved with ISIS were visiting her courses too. Esma says she also ran an internet café for women in the same space, mainly visited by foreign ISIS women – some also Dutch. She pointed this out to the officer. But some of these local ISIS women came mainly to spy on the others, she believes. 'I did not have any real contact with them. They tried to challenge me by talking about politics. When they were in the internet hall, I motioned to the women that they should choose their words with caution.'

The hisba decided that the internet café had to be shut down and increased its patrols. 'Normally I started at nine o'clock until ten o'clock at night. Now I did not open until two o'clock because I was being harassed so much. The hisba checked the tiniest of details. Some of them were polite, but others sneaked up the outside stairs. I put my son there, and when he caught them, he threatened to make a complaint. Soon afterwards I stopped all together.'

Somewhat later, in the year before the liberation, ISIS became more suspicious about the population. Who was giving all kinds of information to the Iraqi army, the Kurds and the Americans? 'Female hisba officers checked the women, to see if they had a sim-card hidden in their headscarf, or in the hem of their dress or sleeve. If they found something, execution would follow.' Esma motions along her throat.

Along with the recognizable hisba, there was also the secret service, the amnia, which mainly operated in civilian clothing. In Mosul, those officers usually worked as taxi drivers. Esma tells me how her aunt, a woman in her seventies, came in conflict with one of them. 'She had just picked up her money and had to hand over a percentage of this to Daesh. Angrily she got into a taxi where she started swearing at Daesh. The driver was with the amnia. These guys did not have long beards, but instead short and neatly trimmed ones. They misled people into speaking freely. He dropped her off in front of the hisba office and purposely dropped her shopping in a puddle of water. She screamed and cried. Because she was an old woman, they let her go.'

+++

In search of more stories about the lives of women in Mosul, I walk into the Erbil office of an Arabic organization that helps women from there. It occupies a tiny office in a large, expensive building from a political organization, because in Iraq everything is political, including help for women.

Lamia Aldabbagh from Source of Life is herself from Mosul

and has been returning regularly to visit her local team since the liberation. 'Mosul has changed after three years under Daesh,' she explains. 'There are so many problems. Not only the Yazidi and Christian women are suffering. All women lost their jobs and had to wear those terrible clothes. And at least three hundred women were murdered, because they were politicians or journalists.'

She considers it her job to document the violence committed against women by ISIS. She spoke to women who had been whipped because they had forgotten to wear their gloves, who needed stitches after being punished with the biter, who had broken an arm or a leg because they had fallen due to the triple layer of fabric from the niqaab blocking their view.

'I met a woman who was punished by having a piece of her tongue cut off. There were small children playing outside her house, and she called out and asked them to leave. The hisba was passing by and heard her voice. They said that a loud voice is haram for a woman.'

Haram, forbidden, or what is actually meant here: in violation with the faith as it is interpreted by ISIS. Women accused of adultery were killed in public by stoning. 'People were forced to watch. Some of the stones were cement blocks. I have seen videos of this on YouTube, but when an eyewitness tells you what they have seen, it is far worse.'

What were the subsequent consequences when violence against women has been approved by those in charge? In the camps where I visit those displaced from Mosul, I am told by aid workers that violence against women is a major problem there. But is also taboo and therefore requires a cautious approach. I know that domestic violence increases under the influence of traumas – and everyone in Mosul has been left traumatized by the cruelties of life under the control of ISIS and the subsequent violence during the liberation. But is that the only reason? If you know how Yazidi women were abused as sex slaves, what does it say about relationships between men and women? Aldabbagh maintains that if the women in Mosul were sexually abused, they would not talk about it. So how can you then find the facts?

I talk to aid workers who work in a camp housing mainly families from Hawija, an important ISIS stronghold, and they tell me that sexual violence is a major problem there. They struggle with it, as discussing it is not possible. And therefore, they are unable to do anything about it.

There is a clear relationship between domestic violence and ISIS. I discover that nearly all of the supporters who have blown themselves up in suicide attacks in Europe, abused their wives at home, a fact that hardly got any media attention. They were frustrated, searching for total control. This begins at home and targets their wives. It appears to be fertile ground for recruiting, violence breeds violence.

It is all too clear that something is going on in Iraq too. And it's not just about arranged marriages for the fighters. During ISIS, relationships between men and women have come under pressure. In one of the camps for displaced persons, I meet sixteen-year-old twins Thoha and Satcha, both wearing coloured headscarves in various shades of blue. Coming from a village, they were left stranded in Mosul without their parents when ISIS took over control. They spent the past three years being terrified. Thoha does the talking, since her sister is suffering from psychological problems and is in bad shape. 'Her hair is falling out. She has been inside for too long worrying about what might happen.'

They were afraid that ISIS would consider them infidels since their village is located in Kurdish territory. And therefore, they were especially fearful of being deemed prey and forced into a marriage, or even worse: that the same fate as the Yazidi women awaited them. They felt trapped. 'My dream is to see my parents. We could not phone them, we had no reception and kept hearing stories that if they found your phone you would be killed. We knew that people who tried to escape at night lost their lives due to the booby traps.'

In a society where honour is so important, the way ISIS views women leads to fear. Would the group really claim possession of women, as they did with the Yazidis? As it deemed it unacceptable for women to stay unmarried, stories circulated about ISIS forcing those women to marry its fighters. I hear these rumours from my adoptive family as well.

According to Sara Mohammed Said (26), an aid worker with the UN organization UNFPA, these are not just stories. In a bare prefab office unit in one of the camps she tells me how her life has changed. Shortly before the occupation began, she divorced and started working for an organization for orphaned children. 'Before Daesh, my father supported me, and I could do what I wanted. But when we realized that they could marry me off to their men, I had to change my lifestyle. I have actually seen it happen to a Syrian girl.'

She talks about the concept of *jihad al nikah*, the holy war through marriage which ISIS imposed on single women and that of the *sabiya*, the slaves. 'It is the same thing, only they were very cruel to the Yazidi women,' she says. 'They had an office in our neighbourhood where we would hear those poor women scream.'

The population knew what was happening to the Yazidis and initially offered resistance. Said's brother saw a young Yazidi woman from his garden. 'He was caught when he offered to contact her family on her behalf. He was whipped.' After the liberation I am told about a number of cases in which the women were hidden by residents of Mosul.

This could not have been easy, since ISIS had many informants among the local population. This is also how they found out where the single women lived, Said explains. Soon she and her three children (the oldest a ten-year-old girl, a highly sought after prey) went into hiding with family members located in another neighbourhood.

When ISIS showed interest in a woman, refusal was impossible. 'I know of a woman that ISIS wanted for a jihad al-nikah. Her father refused. They arrested him along with his son, and then they forced them to work in the construction of tunnels. The woman was also arrested but was later released.' Women who refused a relationship with ISIS were punished, and sometimes even executed on fictitious charges.

She says that women who were forced into a marriage with

an ISIS fighter were taken to Syria, 'where they had a difficult life. No contraception, having one child after the other...'

The jihad al-nikah is not a formal marriage; it can take place after paying a mere 200 dollars to an ISIS judge, with the man placing his hand on the head of the woman and stating that she now belongs to him. There are stories about women being passed around amongst fighters, similar to the Yazidi women being bought and sold for amounts that in August 2016 had reached 1500 dollars per 'slave'.

Many single women remained indoors out of the fear of a forced marriage. Some of them have stated that ISIS sent proposals of marriage, especially for second and third wives. But some cases are known of ISIS men would come home with a Yazidi woman as a sex slave, leading to the departure of their wife with the children in anger and disgust.

Human rights organization Human Rights Watch concluded in a report about gender-related violence under ISIS, that the Sunni women who were the victim of this kind of violence usually remained silent about it, and their families too. They wanted to protect the reputation of the woman, and to prevent that she would be stigmatized, according to HRW. Assistant Manager for the MiddleEast Lama Fakih also reported that 'little is known about the sexual abuse of Sunni women living under ISIS control.'

One of the few examples in the report pertains to a 26-year-old woman from Hawija, the ISIS bastion that at the time this long read was written, still was under the control of the group. The city has been known for many years for its large numbers of supporters of groups such as Al-Qaida and later ISIS. The young woman mentioned, had wanted to marry her cousin, but when he joined ISIS, her parents refused the marriage. In January of 2016, the same cousin forced her to marry him and then raped her.

When she managed to escape to the near-by oil city of Kirkuk, which was under the control of the Kurds, she was eight months pregnant. The child died a few days after the birth.

'Some women try to hide a rape from their own families

fearing being stigmatized, or even to be punished by their family members or the community,' an aid worker for HRW stated. 'Babies born from rape or a forced marriage, carry a stigma.'

+++

To keep their teen-aged daughters out of the greedy hands of ISIS, many mothers married them off to a member of the family. As a result of the occupation, the trend to marry off daughters at an ever-younger age that was visible elsewhere in Iraq too, was accelerated in Mosul.

According to Amina Saleh, a 27-year-old engineer I meet at her parents' home in East-Mosul, poverty also plays a role. Some girls were married off because there was no food left at home, she says. Especially amongst displaced persons, who fled from other Sunni cities to Mosul - first for ISIS fighters and later for the Iraqi army – there is a high number of child and teenage marriages.

Saleh had not been outside for three years, because she absolutely refused to wear a niqaab. When I meet her, she is wearing a white dress with black stripes and tight jeans, with a grey scarf draped loosely over her hair. By offering young women lessons at home, she managed to stay informed. And also, because her father, a public servant who was left unemployed and without any income by ISIS, reported to her what was happening outside her field of vision. Despite an ISIS family living right next door, she and her father regularly took the risk of passing along information to a foreign television station. 'After such an interview, I was unable to sleep at night,' she said.

She witnessed that many girls in her neighbourhood were preparing for a marriage. 'I tried to convince them not to marry at such a young age. Some of them listened to me.' Each case mattered to her, as she cared especially about their development. 'They give up school and their studies. Sometimes I see such a girl, with a young child in her arms and pregnant with another. Some go to school, taking the baby along. It is very sad. Their children are the next generation of Daesh, because their mothers have nothing to teach them since they are uneducated.' That's why Saleh still attempted to educate these young mothers in some way. 'But that is difficult. Their in-laws usually do not want them to become any smarter…'

One of the mothers who arranged such early marriages for her daughters is Badria Hassan (42), who has seven children and fled from Mosul during the liberation. In 2014, soon after ISIS took over the city, she married off two of her daughters to family members. They were eleven and fifteen. 'I was afraid for Daesh and what could happen. It was better to have them safely married. I would not have done it if Daesh had not come. Many other mothers were doing it too.'

Her oldest daughter resisted, she says, but the youngest considered it all very romantic. Yet when I meet Hassan in a camp for displaced persons, it is the youngest one she is most concerned about. 'She is pregnant and cries all the time. I have to go there, even though my house is in ruins. Her husband was arrested by Daesh, and she is now staying with her mother-in-law.'

In search for more information, I meet with researchers from the aid organization Oxfam in Erbil. They also found that the number of teenaged marriages increased under ISIS. Parents told them that they wanted to protect their youngest daughters by marrying them off to a cousin. A remarkable fact from the report, *Gender and Conflict Analyses in ISIS affected Communities of Iraq*, is that due to a lack of suitable marital candidates, parents even chose to place their daughters into a polygamist marriage. 'Becoming a second wife is apparently preferable to becoming the wife of an ISIS fighter,' according to researchers Luisa Dietrich and Simone Carter.

Teenage marriages were not only taking place to keep girls out of the clutches of ISIS, but also to intentionally put them there. According to the Oxfam investigation, young girls were often forced to marry if their fathers, brothers or uncles had joined ISIS. They were the pawn to ensure that their family would have access to an income, services and safety through this close connection with ISIS. I also hear this from Mays in my adopted family in Mosul. 'If their parents were with Daesh, they refused to marry them to normal men,' she explains these kinds of marriages.

The Oxfam researchers also conclude after ISIS there is generally much more pressure on women to marry. The 27-year-old unmarried Amina Saleh is an exception; her highly educated father left her with the choice. But in many families, any unmarried woman over the age of twenty is seen as being not appropriate, and even as a danger to the honour of the family.

3

LOSING YOUR HUSBAND TO ISIS

Under ISIS, thousands of people were executed in Mosul; there were public executions on nearly a daily basis. In particular, those who were police officer before the occupation or soldier in the Iraqi army fell victim to this. Outside of Mosul, a mass grave had been discovered with hundreds of their corpses. Losing your husband during a time of occupation makes daily life even more difficult.

In my adopted family, two members who had been with the police managed to flee from the city, but the son of Syria, one of the older sisters, was arrested and executed. Syria had already lost a son who had been shot and killed years earlier by ISIS' predecessors Al-Qaida. Her third son, who like his brothers was a police officer, went underground and survived.

When I meet Syria in East-Mosul, she is in a wheelchair. Pictures of the murdered sons are passed from hand to hand. Two of her grandchildren, the youngest a baby born during the occupation, are named after them. Syria asks for my help with her health problems, which have become worse since ISIS used her as a human shield, causing her to live in total fear for days as bombs fell nearby. When I promise to find suitable medicine for her swollen legs, a nephew takes me aside. 'My aunt refuses to take her medication since the death of her son,' he says softly. 'Don't trouble yourself with this.'

For a mother, the loss of a son is unbearable, but how do women survive the loss of their husbands? In Mosul, aid worker Lamia Aldabbagh takes me to see two sisters who both experienced this. We walk through the gate, behind which a generator is loudly rumbling to power a washing machine. The smell of bread is dominant; the thin dough is stuck to the sides and baked in a traditional stone oven. The noise of the generator makes our discussion difficult, but when it is turned off the sudden silence is almost as intruding.

Zeineb (31) and Rua (27) have moved in with their mother and grandmother, along with a total of seven children, after ISIS killed their husbands. Both men were arrested because they were in the Iraqi army. Despite signing a document to buy their safety, stating they regretted their actions after Mosul was seized, both men were executed. Their family was unable to give them a funeral; ISIS dumped their bodies in the Khasfa, a deep natural gorge outside of the city that has in fact become a mass grave.

Since then, the sisters have tried to survive. During the occupation they baked bread to sell and crocheted clothes. Stacks of crocheted children's dresses in bright colours and various sizes are taken out of the closet and presented. The grandmother jokes: 'This is what Daesh taught us.'

The hadjia, as the women lovingly call her - the title for a woman who has been on pilgrimage to Mecca – is an inspirational woman. She makes every effort to find the silver lining around all dark clouds. It is a house for women, where despite all the problems, there is still much laughter. I understand just how desperate the situation is, when Zeineb bursts into tears. 'Everyone writes about our story but gives us nothing.' These are the moments a journalist feels like a cruel nosy parker, and I decide not to go away without leaving something behind.

Zeineb says that eleven people are living off the hadjia's

pension. 'My son, who is still going to school, works sometimes.' Their budget is 630.00 dinar per month (not even five hundred euro), and the rent is already four hundred thousand, she says.

Normally in Iraq, the family of the deceased father takes over the care for the children, but not in their case, Rua tells me. 'My mother-in-law came over. She declared that the children were not theirs. Previously there had not been any problems; my husband was even at their house when he was arrested. But they opposed our marriage, they didn't love me.'

When she goes on, I understand just how realistic the fear is amongst widows and single women to be forced into a marriage with an ISIS fighter or supporter. 'Daesh let all of the families in Mosul know that widows of Iraqi soldiers had to remarry,' Rua says. 'They had a procedure in which the man would lay his hand on the head of the woman and say: now I marry you. That's it. An Algerian came to our neighbourhood looking for a wife amongst the widows and divorced women. We hid ourselves.' Apparently, she is referring to the jihad al-nikah, which is a far less formal procedure than a normal marriage which takes place before an ISIS sharia judge.

'We were really afraid,' Zeineb adds. Elsewhere in the street, the ISIS fighter found the widow of a hisba member who agreed to such a marriage. 'He promised her that if he did not die, he would take her away to somewhere else. That is what happened.'

I wonder if it wouldn't be better for the sisters to remarry, knowing the difficulties of single women in Iraq. Zeineb: 'We do not want another husband'. Her mother says that men regularly come to the gate, to ask for their hand. She points to the chubby Rua, whose posture is to the liking of many Iraqi men: 'They especially want her. But she refuses.'

What does their future hold for them? Rua: 'I am waiting for the help of God, what else can I do?' Her sister: 'There is no future for us.' Their mother shakes her head. 'But I do want my daughters to have a future!'

+++

My adopted family also has plenty of stories about what ISIS did to the families of police officers. Various family members tell me about the fate of a distant family member, who was married to a police officer. He fled the city, after which ISIS forced his wife to appear before the sharia court to divorce him. They picked her up twice from her home, but she twice managed to delay a marriage with a man they had found for her. Eventually, the liberation was her salvation from an unwanted marriage.

The loss of a husband is traumatic, but that is also true for the thought of losing him. I meet Rua Khanin (27) in her apartment on the third and highest floor in a semi high-rise neighbourhood in Mosul. Her sons Rami (8) and Aws (4) listen too while hanging around the mainly empty living room. Then Rami takes baby sister Ashwah from her crib and hands her to his mother to feed her a bottle of milk. For she no longer has any milk herself, she says, as the production stopped when ISIS questioned her about the whereabouts of her husband - the baby was only a month old then.

Her husband, Ahmed, was in the army and had fought against ISIS in Ramadi. First his brother Ali was arrested, who also had been in the army. He was accused of spying for the Americans. A few days later he was dead. 'We were afraid, because they followed my husband everywhere. I always had the feeling that there was a car following us. And a year after Ali, they came for him.'

She and her husband went into hiding at various addresses. But ISIS found Rua at her in-laws, and subsequently interrogated her. She knew one of the men, as he came from the same neighbourhood. He had been spying on them. 'I screamed at him, because he was also there when they arrested Ali. I despise him. Then they brought a woman from the hisba to question me, and she beat me on my back and head fifteen times to make sure that I would answer.' Did she know where her husband was? 'Yes, but I didn't tell them and that was really difficult.'

Two of her brothers, who also had been in the army, were arrested and questioned, and then forced to sign a document stating that they would kill her husband if they saw him. There was even an announcement in the mosque, that he was a fugitive and should be caught and executed.

And in the meantime, Rua moved every few days. For a long time, she lived with the uncertainty of her fate, until after the liberation of the first neighbourhood in East-Mosul, when she was reunited with her husband. Then they made contact with the Iraqi army and he gave them all the information he had about ISIS and the locations of their snipers.

The tension did not leave Rua unscathed. 'I am troubled by what has happened. I keep remembering how I was beaten, and it scares me when someone knocks on the door. I keep seeing it all before my eyes. I cannot stand it when my husband is away from home for too long.'

The war left them impoverished. Her husband is now driving a taxi. He would like to join the army again, but it is not accepting any new recruits from Mosul for the present time, 'even though everyone in the army calls him a hero,' she says with obvious pride. 'We have no future: no work, no money. We do not know what is going to happen.'

But she emphasizes that her sister-in-law is far worse off: she was left alone with her young children. 'That is very difficult.' Even though after ISIS, women are once again free to move about, for single women it remains a difficult situation in which they rely on parents and family members. In the conservative society, a woman on her own needs protection and care. Living alone, as is normal in the West, is exceptional here. Because then you will be unprotected from the men who believe you are available for them.

+++

The strong women in my adopted family are all single women. Nidal, who after her divorce moved into the home of her now deceased father to raise her three children on her own, her daughter Hiba, who was studying economics and despite being nearly thirty is still not married, and Syria, who was left alone with her grown sons after the death of her husband. During the occupation by ISIS, they were all forced to turn to male family members for help – sons, brothers, uncles and nephews – to be able to function.

For under ISIS, single women and widows suffer from the simple fact that they are forbidden from being in public without the company of a male family member. For women without a husband, this limits their options to survive in an already complex situation in which they have to care for the family alone. It is therefore not surprising that the investigation by Oxfam reports cases of suicide, citing the example of a widow with two children, who in desperation about being left with no one who takes care of her, decided to drown herself and her children in the river.

And yet the effect can also be positive, the same report concluded, and even lead to a greater role for women. A woman from Anbar told the investigators that especially widows gained more rights in decision making. 'They have become responsible for their families' The women who lost their husbands under ISIS, were forced not only to care for their families but also took on some of the traditionally male tasks, such as decision making.

I notice that Nidal from my adopted family in liberated East-Mosul once again rented a home on her own with her sons and daughter, that became the safe haven for the rest of the family when their neighbourhoods were being liberated. The way she faces life's everyday challenges as a single woman, does not seem to have been affected by ISIS.

4

MARRIED TO THE ENEMY

ISIS has dug its tentacles deep into the society of Mosul. Although much has been written about the foreign fighters who recruited their brides from abroad, far less attention has been paid to local women who married an ISIS supporter. If some twenty percent or even a quarter of the society stood behind ISIS, then part of them would be female. Behind every local fighter there was a woman, sometimes forced into marriage, but sometimes not at all. What kind of women are they?

Little is known about them, but during conversations with women from Mosul, interesting information is revealed about their backgrounds and decisions.

Like when Alya tells me that she would sew clothing on order and advertised this fact via a sign in the yard. It brought the world to her home and sometimes the enemy as well. She recalls a female doctor from a well-known Moslawi family, who asked her face to face what she thought of ISIS. Alya, whose son as a former police officer was forced to flee the city to avoid prosecution, was honest in her reply, despite knowing that the doctor could turn on her: 'I don't like them, because nothing is good now. Business is bad and there is no future. 'The doctor looked at me and said: "Of course you had no problems with the Americans. They didn't take away your son and murder him".'

What a strange coincidence. Alya, who could only just save her son from the clutches of ISIS, was being spoken to by a bitter woman who had lost her son, likely because he was a member of Al-Qaida. He probably was arrested following the American invasion in 2003 and during the hunt for members of the group. That hunt was a success, because Al-Qaida was largely driven out, having fled to Syria when the Americans had to leave Iraq at the end of 2011.

What is it that drives local women to willingly join an organization that is so unfriendly to women as ISIS is? This woman gives us an idea: bitterness about the loss of a husband or child, after which his killer becomes the woman's biggest enemy. It's about revenge towards the enemy. We have seen this in other countries: in Chechnya widows joined radical groups like Al-Qaida and then blew themselves up where it would hurt the Russian enemy most.

Women might even force their husbands to join ISIS, the Oxfam research team discovered. Most probably to be able to survive, as all income had vanished. For instance, a man with three wives was forced to get a job and subsequent income from ISIS. But since he was arrested by the Iraqi army during the liberation of Mosul, the women are now left with nothing at all. Will they regret their choice for ISIS or become bitter about the social rejection that awaits them?

The financial aspect is important, since ISIS wants to make the society dependent. It was a big blow, when in 2015 the Iraqi government halted the payments of civil servants, since an estimated seventy to eighty percent of all incomes in Mosul came from the government. And yet, only a small minority gave in to the enormous financial pressure ISIS put on society. Their salvation were the pensions, which allowed many families to survive for two long years.

Who joined ISIS? Not only people in need of money or the poorly educated. Alya is surprised that people were joining who really should have known better. 'We, as normal people without too much education, did not accept Daesh. But why did the intellectuals believe them?' Others present in the room point out that only a small percentage of the well-educated supported ISIS. But even so, Alya's question is a reasonable one.

From the Oxfam investigation it became evident that the wealthy in the society joined mainly to safeguard their financial position, for example to be able to continue their businesses. Though not forced, the marriages of their daughters with ISIS fighters guaranteed their family safety through a connection with the organization.

Wives of fighters and supporters usually remained in the shadows. But how guilty are they? One of my Iraqi Facebook friends posed that question and received the following answers: 'They eat from the same kitchen, so they are not innocent.' 'They are accomplices.' 'They come from extremist families, from Baathis or Islamists.' 'What choice did the women have? They were forced to do what the son-of-a-bitch wanted.' 'You must judge them on an individual basis.'

Ask that same question in a camp for displaced persons or in Mosul, and the answer will be far less subtle. 'If we see someone who was with Daesh, we will report him,' is the standard answer.

I search of those kinds of women and find two sisters in East-Mosul who both are married to an ISIS fighter. They agree to meet with me and my female translator Lina, in a nearly empty room where they sit on the ground and Lina and myself on the faded green couch. Both women are holding a child on their laps that they cautiously breastfeed under colourful scarves. Although they clearly do not have money, a son is sent out to buy cans of cola for us, since hospitality remains of great importance in Iraq.

They have traded in their niqaab for colourful long dresses; the headscarves that are put back for the photo are removed again after I ask for their story.

Zeineb (31) has five children; her youngest daughter is not yet a year old. Fifteen years ago she married Ayman, who is ten years older than her. He had chosen her as his marital partner when she visited his family to be treated by the father, who reads verses from the Quran and makes charms for the sick.

'I didn't like him, and he was so much older,' she says about her husband, 'but my parents said that I should marry him, for the money.' Her parents did not have money, and neither did she after she married Ayman. 'To earn money, he worked as a carpenter and furniture maker in Erbil.' She points to the wooden show case behind her, as an example of the things he used to make.

'He was good for us. He was not very religious, even though he read the Quran and went to the mosque from time to time. I never imagined that he would become religious one day.'

Rahab (30) met her husband Hassan in her village, just outside of the city of Hamam al-Alil. They fell in love and married, even though his family was not enthusiastic about his choice. 'He was not very religious, and he smoked.' But he did want me to wear the niqaab, 'because he loved me and didn't want others to see me. I did not like it, but eventually I became used to it.'

For both men, the lack of income led them to join ISIS. Hassan was unemployed, and Ayman didn't bring home enough pay from Erbil. 'That he felt drawn to Daesh became evident when he asked me what I thought about him going to work with them,' Rahab tells me. 'Normally he never asked me those kinds of questions. Someone had called him and suggested it. I said that he should refuse, but his mother encouraged him. She said that they were good and that he should join them.'

So here we have a mother who drives her son into the arms of ISIS, even against the wishes of his wife. Rahab's opinion is of no importance, because in Iraqi culture, sons remain loyal to their mothers even after their marriage.

In the case of Zeineb's husband, several cousins had joined, with whom he initially remained in contact without following their example. 'At first, he said it as a joke: "What if I was to join too?"' But when Zeineb asked her brother to give her a few dollars, Ayman became angry. 'He said: "Why are you asking your brother for money? I will give it to you, if it is for yourself."' Apparently, that was the moment when he decided that he needed a better income and that he would get that from ISIS. 'He said: "If I am late tonight, then don't ask where I am."'

Indeed, he did not come home that night. 'We heard that he was at a forty-day training by Daesh. After that he came home. His mother did not accept it, and I said that I wanted a divorce. He said: "You can go, but it's just a job." I was tired, and we did not have any money. I baked bread and made clothes for selling.'

But the money made the difference. 'Daesh paid four hundred dollars when he joined, later five hundred thousand dinars per month, sometimes less.' That was around 350 to 375 euro. 'It is not enough, but my mother often helps me. I stayed with him because I had children.'

ISIS used both men for guard duty, as according to their wives they refused to work for the morality police. Rahab says that her husband, who is known as Abu Raid by ISIS, never had any training. 'My husband was a simple boy. He worked at the check points and refused other jobs with Daesh. Our situation was normal, and to me my husband had not changed.'

But soon, the women start to contradict themselves. Because their husbands had indeed changed. These men, who were barely religious, suddenly started praying five times a day. But that wasn't the biggest change. Ayman, Abu Alaa by ISIS, before joining ISIS was 'a little crazy and often had arguments, but after he was much calmer,' Zeineb says. 'But he complained about headaches and always had red eyes. He asked: "Did you put something in my food? Every time I am here, I have a headache." Even the time that he slept changed.'

It is known that ISIS gave its fighters fear suppressing drugs normally used to treat traumas. Zeineb asks me whether they had put something in her husband's food to make him an addict. The headache could indeed be a sign of withdrawal. But there was more: 'When he came home, he wanted to go back as soon as possible. He had a bag full of medicines, which he took with him once again when he left.' She never got the chance to look into the bag.

Their love life also suffered the consequences, despite his youngest children being conceived during that time. Ayman had a far less desire for sex, Zeineb says. Rahab affirms this for Hassan. 'I said to him: "Don't you love me anymore, because you no longer are sleeping with me?" He did not offer any clear answer.'

And there was another change that put Zeineb's relationship under pressure. She is Shiite, while Ayman is Sunni, just like ISIS. The group portrayed the Shiite majority in Iraq as being infidels. 'When we got married no one cared about that difference. But later on, he said to me: "If I had known what I know now, I would never have married you."'

Ayman is no longer alive, Zeineb only recently discovered. 'I had not heard from him in five months. He was sad, the last time I saw him, because he wanted us to come to West-Mosul when the operation began. But I refused. He died in that battle.'

Rahab's says that her husband joined for a year, 'only because we were hungry. He is with them no longer.' ISIS was not happy about Hassan's departure, and he was put under pressure to return. He went into hiding. 'He left because of the murders and the severe punishments,' Rahab says. And Zeineb confirmed: 'My husband kept complaining: "They kill so fast."'

At the time of the interview, Hassan is in West-Mosul, living with his sister, in an area that has not yet been liberated. He is afraid to return because his name is in the army's database. 'My husband is no longer with Daesh, but he is afraid that he will be killed if he turns himself in to the Iraqi army.'

If he kept out of ISIS' hands, he most probably has been arrested during or after the liberation and given a death sentence for joining a terror group.

The sisters now live in a liberated neighbourhood with their children, where citizens can now openly speak out against ISIS, and that is exactly what they do. And yet the women claim that they do not experience any negative consequences. 'There are no problems with the neighbours,' according to Zeineb. 'During the occupation our situation was the same; we did not feel like we were part of Daesh. The men just wanted to work. My neighbours first allowed me to stay in their own house. No, they are not afraid. My husband did not cause any problems for anyone. They say that he was a good man and ask: why did he join?'

But when I pressure them about what their future, the image becomes much less rosy. Both women now have problems with their families. Zeineb: 'My family has asked me to come to Baghdad and leave the children behind with Ayman's parents. Thanks to Daesh, I have a problem. My in-laws do not want my children, and the kids do not like them either. I do not want to leave them here.'

Rahab says: 'My husband's family rejects me and the children. After the liberation my father-in-law rejected me. They are afraid both of the government and of Daesh.'

Zeineb confesses that she is so desperate she sometimes considers dousing herself with petrol and setting it on fire. 'But I don't do that because of the children. We can no longer pay the rent. A NGO has given us a tent, that we will be forced to use at some point, I'm afraid.'

Then it becomes clear that Zeineb's 13-year-old son Mustafa is having trouble at school: children are cursing at him and calling him Daeshi. And Zeineb asks for my help to repair her old sewing machine, so that she can once again have an income. But how difficult that will be is revealed when Rahab says that she would like to open a beauty parlour. 'But I am afraid that no one will come,' she adds somberly.

The best thing would be, she concludes, to move to a neighbourhood where no one knows them. But that will not happen, 'because we do not have the money.' The women have ended up in a vicious circle.

I decide, against my journalistic ethics, to help them. Along with my translator, I buy a second-hand sewing machine in Erbil of a good brand. Lina sees to it that it ends up with the women in Mosul. 'They are so very happy with it,' she later tells me. I only hope that our contribution can break the circle and offer the women a future.

+++

If these women, who did not ask for any of this, are having such a hard time, how is it for those who made a conscious decision to join ISIS? I go in search of these women, but it's not easy to find them. If they are in the camps, then they hide amongst the other displaced persons and fearfully keep their background secret. I get on the trail of a woman who has gone underground in Erbil, but she will not talk for fear of what the Kurdish security forces would do if they found her. And when she remarries, she has an even better reason to remain silent: her new husband does not know about her past.

Sara Mohammed Said (26) from the UN organization UNFPA, tells me about a woman in the Hasansham camp where she works, who was married to an ISIS guy. That happened via her brother, who had joined the group without the approval of their family, which publicly distanced themselves from him. The brother was killed, just like the woman's husband.

Said suggests that it was a case of forced marriage. 'In the camp they hated her in the beginning, until they realized that she had no choice in the matter,' she says. 'I tried to comfort her by saying that it was not her fault, but I fear for her future, should she want to return to Mosul.'

She is not only referring to the child that the woman has from the ISIS man, but also to the problems she should expect with all official documents she needs. Her marriage and the birth were registered under ISIS; and those documents have been declared invalid since the liberation. The Iraqi court has set up a special office in the camp, where such documents can be exchanged for legitimate Iraqi ones. Said advised the woman to register the child on the name of her parents, as the father was not there anyway.

Unfortunately, she had already left the camp when I spoke to Said, and therefore my search for women with ties to ISIS continued. Especially for women who had agreed to a jihad al-nikah. This marriage as an act of holy war can perhaps be compared to the concept of the comfort women from Asia: women who were forced into prostitution by the occupying troops.

Sometimes the women offered themselves, in order to get some money for example. Esma, whom I meet at my adoptive family from Mosul, also believes that not all women in Iraq were forced into such a marriage. 'Sometimes, it was their father or brother who was with Daesh, and convinced them to get married. Some of these men were then promoted.'

The wives of ISIS fighters know that their men will most likely be killed – they die in battle or are sent on a suicide mission. And then the real problems begin. Once you become a widow, the hunt is on, Esma tells me, clearly gloating over the story. She comes up with a story about a widow who went before the sharia-judge to demand her right to a pension.

'She took along her son, but the judge sent him out of the room,' according to Esma. 'Then he asked her to remove the khimar.' Taking off the niqaab in front of a man who is not a family member, is only possible after marriage according to the strict rules of ISIS. The judge wanted to force her to do just that, to be able to test the goods beforehand. The woman, who saw she was in an impossible position, began to scream loudly, Esma tells me.

'Her son rushed in, and she told him to take her back home, as she no longer even wanted her pension rights. These people are so evil, and they are breaking the Islamic laws.' Esma explains, that according to those laws, a widow must remain home for three months and ten days after the death of her husband to make sure she is not pregnant from him. The same judge later proposed to another widow, who did accept him, she says.

Many of the women moved with their husbands from East to West-Mosul, and then further to Syria, when the battle of the liberation began. And yet that is but one of the many reasons why it is so difficult to find the ISIS women.

According to aid worker Lamia Aldabbagh they simply do not want to be recognized. 'If we record their information, that must be done in secret. It is not like the Yazidi women, since everyone knows about their fate. A Muslim woman cannot talk about this, because Mosul is conservative. Women move from neighbourhood to neighbourhood to keep from being noticed. But if she is alone, and pregnant, then it is hard to hide yourself.'

In Mosul, engineer Amina Saleh reports about a camp for the families of ISIS, outside of Mosul, that is still under construction. And another one is already in use, to the south of the city. Mays from my adopted family believes she passed by that camp, when she had fled to East-Mosul along with her father, brother and sister.

During my search for such a camp, I end up at a police station in Mosul. Because what is the police doing with ISIS women? The man in charge, Colonel Ahmed, sits behind a desk that is located next to a bed with neatly folded blankets – apparently his family is still located outside of the city, and he is therefore sleeping at work. The Karama police station is located in a former school, with a cell with blue-painted bars in which prisoners are held, just behind the entrance. But they are mainly normal criminals, who are suspected of theft and assault. And only sometimes, a lone supporter of ISIS.

Sometimes people come to report that their neighbours were part of ISIS, the colonel says. 'We then investigate this, make a report and send that to the judge.' That is important for those who suffered damages due to ISIS; based on the investigation they can request compensation. A special judge has been appointed in liberated areas, to handle these types of cases.

'If we discover that Daesh is located somewhere, then we go there and arrest him,' Colonel Ahmed says. 'There is no special arrangement; we treat them like normal people.'

What does he know about ISIS families, or women who have gone into hiding, I ask him. 'We have no idea if we have any here,' the colonel says. 'Most of the families went with the fighters to Raqqa in Syria. Some of them are just living here, while others are in the camps. They are families just like all of the others.' He has not yet arrested any women who were with ISIS.

But will I perhaps be able to find them in a camp that has been especially set up for ISIS families? The colonel has disappointing news. There is an urgent need for such a camp, but it has not yet been built. 'There are many people who have lost family members due to Daesh. We are afraid of acts of revenge, problems between the people, of tension. Those people would be safer in such a camp.'

Shortly afterwards, the Kurdish media network Rudaw posts a video on Twitter from such a camp, near the oil city of Kirkuk. It appears a number of women are located here, who were married to men from ISIS, some by force, via a jihad al-nikah. A woman cries and says that she does not know who the father is of her new-born child, because the fighter she had married died and then a jihad al-nikah followed with a commander. All she knows is that the father was an Iraqi, she says. Nothing else. And that she does not want to keep the child.

Another woman appears who has two daughters, that were both married to ISIS fighters. Forced into a jihad al-nikah, she says. One suffered psychological damage, and her mother is now caring for her two children. The other is still with her ISIS husband in Hawija, which will be one of the last towns to be liberated in 2017.

Some ISIS women end up in jail. Thanks to a report by Human Rights Watch I discover that ten of them are being held in Erbil at the Women and Children's Reformatory. They are all suspected of having ties to ISIS, but from the report it is clear that some of them were forced into a marriage, or that their husband only joined ISIS after they had been married for years.

Of the ten women being held at the women's prison, two were accused of planning a suicide attack, with one of them having confessed to this. The other eight said that their only crime was that they had a husband who belonged to ISIS or Al-Qaida. All my attempts to speak to the women myself, unfortunately stranded due to Kurdish bureaucracy.

It is well known that screening centres for displaced persons from Mosul have arrested thousands of men for alleged ties to ISIS. But what about the women? I find an article about thirty foreign ISIS women who were arrested in Mosul, but it fails to report where they are now.

Later still, the families of foreign ISIS fighters are locked up in special prison camps, some in Iraq under the authority of the Iraqi police, some in Syria with the Kurdish forces fighting ISIS there. But most of the local ISIS families from liberated Iraqi cities like Mosul, Talafar and Hawija eventually find refuge in the same IDP camps as non-ISIS civilians who fled the battle for the liberation of those cities.

+++

Why is it so difficult to find a woman who made a conscious choice for ISIS? My conclusion is that it is a taboo. That people in Iraq would rather not discuss the fact that women had joined ISIS from their own free will. People would rather prefer to believe they are instead victims, forced into a marriage or only able to watch helplessly as their husband or son joined; that is also the story that women from ISIS try to convey – as part of their effort to avoid acts of revenge.

And yet this does not necessarily mean that society will welcome the ISIS women and their children. It is only normal that families no longer want anything to do with their daughters-in-laws, like in the case of Zeineb and Rahab.

Even women who only married an ISIS supporter because they were seeking protection as a single woman or a widow, will have a difficult time functioning in society again, aid worker Sara Mohammed Said says.

Engineer Amina Saleh views them as a potential danger. ‘Their heads have been filled by Daesh. They continue to think according to the Daesh ideology. One such woman told me that she would go to Rome,’ she says laughing, referring to the ISIS battle cry that its supporters would soon be conquering Rome. ‘The children need a great deal of care. They are now often with the grandparents, or the mother. Maybe they no longer have a house, and nothing to eat. That's the next generation of Daesh.'

Lamia Aldabbagh from Source of Life suggests that the government is considering keeping ISIS children isolated, due to the danger they might pose. 'We do not want that; the children must be a part of society.'

She expects that the women eventually will get back into the society, despite a multitude of obstacles. For example, for women who are pregnant with a child they now do not want anymore. Registering the birth will cause problems, especially if the father is a foreign fighter and is known only by his kunya or nickname - such as with Ahmed al Hollandi. According to Iraq law, that child receives the nationality of the father.

With the help of two witnesses, the child of such a fighter can be registered under the name of the mother, Aldabbagh says. She also works as an attorney. 'And according to the law, a child of an unknown father may be placed with another family because it is considered to be an orphan.'

Dr. Sabaa Chief, who is in charge of the women's division of the Al-Khanjer Development Foundation in Erbil, is conducting a study about this issue. She is calling for separate neighbourhoods to be established for the ISIS families. There, they must become part of a rehabilitation process, with special schools for the children and treatment for the mothers, to allow them to slowly integrate back into society.

This idea alone reveals just how stigmatized families who had ties to ISIS are - even if it pertained to a distant family member, or a forced marriage. I even hear about a marriage that was called off by the bride's family, because the groom had a distant cousin who was with ISIS.

When I talk about this with displaced persons in Mosul, the message I receive is in unison: we no longer want them. Living next door to someone who was with ISIS is seen as extremely dangerous. 'They must hang them all,' a young man says, who was trapped between the two sides, due to a cousin who was with ISIS. The cousin pressured him to join as well, and although he refused, he was still condemned by the neighbourhood due to this cousin.

To measure these kinds of reactions, I meet up with women from Mosul in Dr. Sabaa's office. I ask teacher Nihaya Mohammed (53) what she would do, if after returning home she discovered that her neighbour, a woman who belonged to ISIS, was still living there. 'I would have to report her; she is a source of fear and likely still has contact with Daesh.'

Wiam Mokhtar (54), who came with her daughter and granddaughter, confirms this. 'Because how can we build a new society if they are still there? If the son was with Daesh, I must be careful.' She speaks from experience, as in 2004 her husband was kidnapped by Al-Qaida, because he allegedly worked with the Americans. He survived after paying a ransom, and the family then moved to Syria only to return in 2011.

When the balance of power changed, following the arrival of Iraqi troops, women in various Iraqi cities asked for a divorce, to try to conceal their ties to ISIS. However, society does not view this as a means of distancing themselves from the detested group. It fails to help them polish up their tarnished reputations, Aldabbagh says. According to her, some women simply tear up their marital contracts to hide the fact that they were married to an ISIS fighter. 'The government does not even accept the Daesh contracts, but the paper is needed to give the woman a new, official document.'

Many women will not want to do this, because if it becomes known that their ISIS husband has disappeared or died, they will then be in danger of being raped or sexually abused. They know the ever-present threat of revenge all too well and are acutely aware of the danger when men discover there is no longer a man to protect them.

Following previous conflicts in Iraq, the perpetrators and their families resettled in areas where no one knew them, and in some cases even changed their names to conceal their past. It appears that governing bodies in Iraq are once again steering in this direction. In the Iraqi provinces of Salahadin and Babylon not only has the right of ISIS-families to return been revoked, their possessions have also been confiscated. The only exception to this is for families who have voluntarily handed over a family member who had ties to ISIS. Human Rights Watch has protested against this measure, since families often have no control over their sons' decisions to join ISIS. The result is that both for ISIS families, and for women who were married to an ISIS fighter or supporter, it has become uncertain where they will be able to relocate.

The involved governing bodies have stated efforts will be made to divert attempted acts of retaliation. But they are in fact creating a new problem as the measure will only increase poverty, bitterness, and lead to frustration and aid in the emergence of an 'ISIS 2.0'. This conclusion can be reached from the simple fact that ISIS' supporters in Mosul were for the most part villagers from the countryside, who ended up being displaced due to government measures and wars and subsequently settled in the city. They were not welcome there, did not integrate well and ended up at the lowest level of society – which created fertile ground for groups like Al-Qaida and later ISIS.

And these acts of retaliation are already taking place. In Qayyara for instance, there is a small group of houses which have been looted and now stand empty; where judging from the writing on the fence, this was an act of retaliation because the residents were with ISIS. Aldabbagh also says that if a neighbourhood discovers a family there had ties to ISIS, they will be evicted, and the house burned to the ground.

The result is a divided society where feelings of revenge and bitterness prevail. Where people reject one another, feel like victims and wish death upon their culprits. How can a city survive, and in particular its women, in such an extreme situation where a next conflict seems inevitable?

5

AFTER ISIS

The implications for the lives of women after ISIS go much further than having difficulty in making ends meet or wanting a divorce because you married far too young. When I am invited to participate in a new Arabic think tank for a discussion in Erbil about the future of Mosul, one thing is immediately blatantly obvious: I am the only woman. More than twenty men are giving speeches about what should happen to stabilize Mosul, with some even insisting upon a military regime. Important matters such as restoring trust and improving the situation of women, who have suffered so much under ISIS, are not even discussed.

Am I the only woman, because ISIS had executed several hundreds of politically-active women from Mosul? Likely not. Nor can the fact that life in the camps demands so much improvisational capacities that women no longer have time for politics hardly be the reason that the think tank did not include them. No, even before ISIS, it would have been exceptional to find women in these kinds of positions.

At the same time, many of the aid workers in the camps for displaced persons are Arabs and female, and women like aid worker Lamia Aldabbagh and Dr. Sabaa manage to lead their own organizations. And haven't the women from the Barzani tribe, just like more recently the Yazidi women, proven that under pressure everything becomes fluid, and that's when these women go through a process of development?

What people try to do, following a disaster such as with ISIS, is to return to the status quo as soon as possible. But this is not possible, because this disastrous period has left its mark. People have lost loved ones. Lost three years of their lives. Witnessed their homes being turned into rubble. And they were forced to adapt to the new situation.

The relationships between men and women, even within a marriage, were also greatly affected by ISIS. Think about Esma, who told me how her husband, before they would go outside, checked her from top to toe to make sure that he wouldn't get into trouble. Because ISIS also punished the husband with lashes if his wife had a hole in her sock or had forgotten her gloves. They made men responsible for the actions of their wives, as if they were no longer capable of making any decisions on their own. How accustomed to this would one become, in three years' time?

In Mosul I speak to the English teacher Muammar Yousif, who is in his twenties and tells me that at one point he refused to go outside anymore with his mother. Because he had no patience for the criticism of the hisba and due to this he was placing them both in harm's way. But also, because he felt forced to comply with a rule of ISIS which he loathed. He refused to allow himself to be led by fear, to do something he did not agree with in the first place. There were not many like him. Most men walked straight into the trap ISIS created for them.

The punishments they received due to their wives were carried out in public and were very humiliating, which was the source of tension within the families. The Oxfam researchers quoted a male displaced person, who said that 'in three years,

ISIS had controlled everything and spoiled the relationships between a husband and wife'.

A female respondent told the researchers that her husband used ISIS to control her. 'He always said: "If you don't keep quiet, I will tell Daesh that you are not a good wife and that they may take you away."'

Will what has become a habit in three years' time, simply just disappear? I think not. The Oxfam researchers saw a promise in the changed balance, and a reason to put extra effort into changing the roles between men and women in a positive sense. But the society was already a conservative one before ISIS arrived, so I doubt if it will be possible to improve something in this current situation that under normal circumstances takes a long process – the improvement of the position of women.

When you walk through liberated Mosul, you will see that the situation from before ISIS is recovering. The shopkeepers are men once again; their wives and daughters who handled the sales inside to women, have disappeared. Although in some neighbourhoods there are hardly any women in the streets, you can see them with their children in the evenings, at shopping malls and ice cream parlours. Hairdressers and beauty parlours have once again opened their doors. Women wear cheerful scarves, but short sleeves and skirts above the knee still are unaccepted in the public domain.

Something else is going on as well. From the camps for IDPs reports came in about high levels of domestic violence. But I discover that this was already happening during the occupation too. The Oxfam report says that a growing number of people remained home due to the collapse of social structures, since under ISIS one had no idea whom to trust, along with the lack of safe public spaces. Also, the fear because of the loss of family members who had been murdered and the strict clothing laws played a role in keeping people indoors. All this led to tensions, especially within the family. In that pressure cooker of a home you could hardly leave, the man often took his frustration about not having a job or any income out on his wife. ISIS controlled the economy. In an attempt to restore their masculinity, many men dealt with the pressure of having to care for and protect their families, and their growing inability to do so, by abusing their wives, the Oxfam researchers concluded.

A result of this is an increase of the number of suicides of women who see that as the only way of escaping the on-going abuse. Divorces are mentioned less often; it remains a controversial topic in the conservative society of Mosul. And the fear of attracting the attention of ISIS as a divorced woman and being forced into a new marriage, also plays an important role.

In Dr. Sabaa's office I ask Wiam and her daughter Rima what effects the three-year occupation has had on them. Rima (25) says that both she and her husband were forced to quit their studies. That he had opened a clothing shop to support the family, which ISIS then confiscated. Now they are left with nothing, no study and no income. 'I am supported by my father-in-law who is still in Mosul,' she says, while trying to keep her toddler daughter from snitching my water bottle.

'I could feel that time stood still, and that I had no future,' schoolteacher Nihaya adds to the conversation. She was not allowed to teach under ISIS. 'But now I feel that there is hope. My children are back in school and at university, and I am teaching the displaced.'

She says that she is proud of the fact that during the occupation she was successful in sending her son to the Kurdish region to study. That is an example of the positive aspects, that I am happy were also there. Although women did indeed remain home, they found themselves being forced into taking on other roles than they were used to. The two sisters living with their mother and grandmother, baked bread and made children's clothing to sell, Esma organized knitting classes and opened an internet café for women to generate an income, and Amina taught young women. They all used their creativity to help ensure that they would survive.

Sometimes roles would change. Since children were forced to remain home from school, women had to pay more attention to their upbringing. There are families that chose to home school their children, which meant the children after the liberation needed only a year to catch up instead of two.

The role of women was also important in preventing their children from being recruited. If their sons felt attracted to the ISIS ideology, they had to offer some counterweight. I know for certain that many more teenagers would have joined ISIS, if their mothers had failed to dissuade them or talked them out of it in a sensible manner.

Oxfam concluded that some women, after having their husbands killed by ISIS, were forced into the role of decision maker in the household. Normally this would be a task of the husband. Even in the camps for displaced persons, women admit that the decision to flee or to return home was not theirs, but the husband's. Women who were forced to survive without a husband became responsible for their families. In extreme cases – in some remote villages outside of Mosul – they even used weapons to defend themselves from attackers, whether ISIS or not.

And yet the shift is also evident in families where the husband is still present. The Oxfam researchers speak of 'bonding', due to the mutual suffering of the couple under ISIS, which had led to more decisions being made jointly. And a number of those being interviewed also stated that even now women were the ones making most of the decisions in the household: 'They check the expenditures and the budget, and they have the power to make decisions about everything that affects their children, such as marriage, health and education.'

That can explain the men's frustrations, as they are feeling the power slipping away from them. The Oxfam investigation reveals that this will likely not be a permanent situation. Because the men oppose it. Women should not interfere with decisions about how money is being spent in the home, they feel, and must 'be patient and obedient and support and help their husband (..) because the man needs a soft woman who is patient'.

That think tank in Erbil most likely did not even consider applying a percentage of women to participate in their meeting

– as is commonplace in many Western countries. ‘Women in our society are absent in decision making and problem solving, because we are accustomed to the men making the decisions,’ a female interviewee said to Oxfam. But when the researchers asked the displaced women from Mosul if they could see a role for themselves in problem solving once they returned home, three-quarters responded with yes.

An interesting factor in this, is also the changing role of the mother-in-law due to the occupation. In my conversations with women in Mosul I keep hearing about husbands who beat a path to their mothers’ door, and for important decisions chose to listen to their mother instead of their wife. Like the example of the police officers who returned out of hiding and then signing a declaration of remorse because the mother wants them to, even if the wife was justifiably cautious in doing so. Yet, due to families being forced to rely on themselves more often under ISIS, and the limited contract with the in-laws, the power and influence of the mother-in-law also diminished, Oxfam concluded.

As is clear from schoolteacher Nihaya’s case, not only men lost their jobs under ISIS. The big question remains, whether women will soon be allowed to return to work. Even if the need is there since an income is necessary, for many women this will depend on their husbands having a job again. Because only when the gender balance is restored, the fact that she has work, will not be an attack on his masculinity.

Knowing this, I wonder how permanent the changes in the families will be after three years under ISIS. How quickly will the balance in marriages return? And in society? Because there are now more widows than there would normally be, more women who married young and in doing so lost the opportunity to study, and more women left without work than before.

And just as important is the fact that society has lost its social context. That contact between people was lost, as a result of everyone being isolated. And this in turn has led to distrust and uncertainty.

+++

When you ask women about their future, then it is all about safety and trust. An expression of this is for example the number of niqabs still being worn in the streets. This is leading to distrust amongst women who eagerly cast off the 'black bitch' or use it as a mop to do the floors. For who would want to continue to wear that oppressive piece of clothing, unless you are with ISIS?

My adopted niece Mays tells me about this. 'I see those women and am reminded about Daesh. Daesh forced all women to wear a khimar, but it is not obligatory in our faith, it is your personal freedom. We do not trust them, those women who are still wearing a khimar.'

Aid worker Lamia Aldabbagh speaks to women she meets in Mosul about this. 'We suggest removing the khimar, to show that we are able to speak freely. That is the first step we must take: convincing women that it is no longer necessary.'

I can see the need for this at a girl's school I visit in East-Mosul. The students tell me that they too are distrustful about women out in the streets who are still wearing a niqaab. 'I feel sick when I see them,' Mumtar says (19). 'Before Daesh there were not many women who wore one and they now take them off because they do not want to be seen as Daesh.' Distrust is also evident towards the wives of ISIS members. 'Some of those women were in the hisba, but they were hiding behind the niqaab, so how will we be able to recognize them now?' asks Ayat (18).

Not long after, the government in Mosul announces a ban on wearing the niqab. This is mainly for security reasons; to prevent suicide attackers from being able to go unnoticed in busy areas disguised as a woman. But this will also have an effect on society. One reason to harbour feelings of distrust has been removed. And even more importantly: the most oppressive symbol of the control by ISIS is banned.

Aldabbagh sees it as her work to attempt to rehabilitate the women of Daesh. 'We must tear down the wall of fear,' she concludes, while sombrely adding that there is time nor money to achieve this.

When you talk to women, often you realize just how difficult that will be, and how embedded the fear and distrust have become. Esma says that she no longer trusts anyone in Mosul. 'Daesh is not leaving. There are many people who supported them but never revealed it. There can be sleeping cells.'

What does she base this on? 'The last Friday before the liberation, the imam in the mosque said that the Shiites would come and rape all the women. That they refer to Moslawi-women as "white meat".'

The Iraqi army that liberated Mosul was largely made up of Shiites, just like the militias fighting ISIS outside of the city. Despite the scare campaign of ISIS, most of the civilians welcomed them with open arms and celebrations.

My adopted family also does not want to hear anything negative about them. 'Before the army came, Daesh said that the Shiites would take our women and homes, but we only saw the complete opposite,' Nasser said angrily. 'There is no difference between Sunnis and Shiites, it was Daesh making that difference.'

Esma says that the same imam who spoke of 'white meat', threatened revenge upon anyone cooperating with the army. It failed to impress, and Esma too promises that they will go down fighting: 'I am angry and afraid, but prepared to give all the information I have so that all of Daesh can be locked up.'

The seeds of fear have been sown very deliberately. From various sides, I hear about ISIS-imams and fighters who told the population they would return. In the girl's school, Ayat mentions a member of ISIS coming into her brother's shop. 'He said that they would never leave Mosul, because it is their capital.' Amina (20): 'A month after the liberation, explosions began; how is that possible if members of ISIS are not hiding here?'

Rua Khanin, who went into hiding because her husband was being sought, said that when her brothers were arrested to get hold of him, they were told that ISIS supporters were expecting to return, but as a different militia. Her mother too had the fear put into her. 'A few days ago, she was walking with another woman on the street. Someone stopped in front of them. It was a teenager who said: "Now you are walking without a khimar, eh? Just wait until we are back!"'

Schoolteacher Nihaya explains what that fear of ISIS' return is based upon. 'Before we had Daesh, there was Al-Qaida, with kidnappings and extortion. We are afraid that this will be repeated, because they are still here, now as sleeper cells.' Because these types of radical groups were previously active as criminal organizations 'we do not believe that we will ever be rid of them.'

She admits to having become cautious in how she deals with people, because she no longer knows whom she can trust. 'We wonder if Mosul will ever be as safe as Erbil again. That is because of the suicide bombers.' ISIS manages to get its supporters to blow themselves up in liberated neighbourhoods, on busy locations such as restaurants or schools.

The threat affects their lives, she says. 'People are preoccupied with it, they are afraid. I am concerned that the security forces will not be able to gain control of the situation.'

But the fear is also related to those same security forces, to the police and Shiite militias. In the camps for displaced persons, sexual intimidation is reported by the military towards young women. They arrest male family members based on false allegations, to be able to exert pressure on the women to submit to their sexual advances.

Other reports say that Iraqi soldiers are looting abandoned homes in Mosul. And even worse, they allow themselves to be bribed by members of ISIS. 'When civilians report that a house belonged to Daesh, or someone who was a member of the group, then the military sometimes says: that is not our job,' Aldabbagh says. 'Or they arrest the person, who is then released within a day or two.'

Colonel Ahmed of the Mosul police does not agree. 'We have discovered some Daesh sleeper cells, but people from

Mosul have the tendency to exaggerate things. Yes, we are still finding Daeshi. Sometimes we can get some information, such as yesterday when we arrested two brothers. Whoever we find, is sent on to the judge in Hamdaniya.' In this liberated Christian city, a court has been established where the charges against members of ISIS are formulated.

Women who were with ISIS have not yet been arrested, he says. So my search for them continues.

+++

While in Baghdad on reportage, this search suddenly gets pushed into the right direction. Thanks to Hanaa Edwar, an agile and alert 70-year-old Iraqi who leads the Al-Amal Association. It is working in the camps for displaced persons and is one of the few NGO's, she tells me, active in the Shahama camp, just outside of Tikrit, where more than 350 ISIS families are locked up, who came from the former Iraqi ISIS bastion Shargat and some from the still occupied Hawija.

So a legitimate camp for ISIS families really does exist, and I can even reach it in three hours from Baghdad. Edwar helps me, as one of the first journalists, to gain access. This is quite unique, because the families – especially women and children, but also some married couples and older men – are totally cut off from the outside world, with no visitors and no access even to phones.

'They are afraid that we will pass along information to Daesh,' Samara Musa (35) tells me, who lives in a tent in the camp, along with nine children. Since she is not allowed to have a phone, for some time now she has not received any news about her husband, who was arrested by the Iraqi army. 'Because his brother was with Daesh,' she says. The brother is now with ISIS in Syria. 'We had arguments with him. We were not part of Daesh, and we also received nothing from them.'

This is what the majority of the women tell me, during the few hours I was able to spend in the camp: a son, husband, father or brother joined, the families opposed this but were left powerless and are now being punished. The detained family members feel they are victims, although most do admit to initially being happy with the arrival of ISIS. However, now they say they had realized within months what the group was really about.

In all my interviews, this feeling of being a victim is revealed. 'I don't even have the money to buy a kilo of tomatoes,' Saheya Ibrahim complains. This woman who says she is 'somewhere in the fifties', is in the camp with her husband. They tried in vain to stop their son, when he wanted to join ISIS, just as his uncle – her brother. Where they are now, they do not know. Nor do they know the whereabouts of her second son, who was arrested by the army due to his family's ties with ISIS.

I am reminded of reports about the way Iraqi police forces treated the arrestees during the operation to liberate Mosul. Iraqi photographer Ali Arkady published horrific photos and videos about torture and murder. And for some time now, the rumour has been circulating amongst my colleagues in Iraq about members of ISIS who were arrested by the Iraqi police or the army, and after being interrogated were then executed. Human Rights Watch reported that the corpses of men wearing handcuffs and blindfolds had been discovered in a field. They appeared to have been executed on the spot by the Iraqi troops. The organization also revealed details about secret prisons where detainees with a possible connection to ISIS were being held under abominable circumstances, and without being charged or given access to legal counsel.

I discover that Shahama, which opened in January 2017, is not the only camp for ISIS family members in Iraq. Also in Amiriya Fallujah, a town close to Fallujah city, hundreds of families are living who are not allowed to leave the town. And roughly another 170 families are in Laylan camp, near the oil-rich city of Kirkuk; they are mainly women coming from the ISIS stronghold of Hawija, who had been forced into a jihad al-nikah.

Still others fled along with the refugees from Tikrit,

Fallujah and Mosul onto the camps for displaced persons. Some went underground, but more often they are known to the authorities and shunned by other refugees, who had lost family members due to the ISIS regime or the battle against them.

But are there women in the Shahama camp who made a conscious choice for ISIS? When I ask the women here what they think about the group, they are united in their condemnation of it. 'They are infidels,' according to Iman Hazem Ismael (47), a thin widow who saw two of her five sons join ISIS. They were seventeen and twenty then, and were later killed during gunfire by the Iraqi army.

Hazem has traded her black niqaab for a large tiger-print head scarf which also covers her small shoulders and does not match her blue dress with white polka dots. The management of the camp reports that she actively worked with the ISIS regime by conducting body searches on women. ISIS does not permit men to touch women, and they had to be checked when entering buildings or at checkpoints, for example for the illegal possession of SIM cards.

She is aware of the accusation, she says impassively, but it is all nonsense. She claims to have asked her sons to leave ISIS. She was even beaten by ISIS and was threatened with the execution of her other sons after she had attempted to escape.

I would like to believe her, but then she tells me that the baby sleeping next to her in the stifling hot tent is her daughter's, who was married to an emir (a leader) of ISIS. She has fled to Syria with her husband and father-in-law. So next to her two sons who were fighting with ISIS, she also has a daughter who was involved with them. And as family of the fighters, ISIS sent them all to Mosul. When the Iraqi army liberated East-Mosul, ISIS put them on boats across the Tigris to the still occupied western part of the city, where they would eventually surrender to the army. Just how involved are you then?

If she really is a supporter of ISIS, then she is not yet prepared to admit to this. And the only thing I can ascertain from the process that led to her making this choice, is that she, like many other Sunnis, initially viewed ISIS as the salvation from the discriminating regime of the Shiite majority that came into power in Iraq after the fall of Saddam Hussein.

Most of the women complain about the hopelessness of the situation; where can they go? 'I don't think that we will be able to live with the people,' Hazem concludes when asked about her future. 'My oldest son has done too much to too many people. He made a huge mistake.' She is sorry, she says. 'I want to raise my other sons in a different way. I am very tired. I have nothing left.'

The camp has a small school but offers nothing to the older children. And money is a problem. Hazem believes that as a widow whose sons were killed, she should receive benefits. She would like to live somewhere where no one knows her. 'I just want to feel like an Iraqi once more. Here they only call us Daesh families. We have to be rid of that.'

The young generation of my adoptive family in Mosul has told me that there is fear for the supporters of ISIS who have gone into hiding. And that no one knows whether their families can be trusted, because they are perhaps still actively working for the group. After the talk with Hazem, I can fully understand this doubt: is she a victim or a culprit, or both?

Because many people who join ISIS, seemed so normal. 'My manager joined them,' one of the nephews in my adopted family tells me. His cousin Mays adds: 'Due to this, we no longer trust people anymore, we distrust some in our surroundings and even in the family.'

Just how strong the negative feelings are towards the families, becomes apparent when pamphlets are distributed that are addressed at the 'families of Daesh'. 'Your family members have abused this forgiving city and her peaceful, good citizens,' according to the pamphlet which was written using flowery Arabic and begins with a Sura from the Quran. The message is clear: leave, otherwise the families will become targets, 'because we have run out of patience. Do not become the victims of our bullets instead of your wicked sons.'

Who sent this, remains unclear, but it is a known fact

that in the months following the liberation numerous groups are actively seeking revenge against those who they view as being supporters of ISIS. And the same goes for their families.

This hatred even reaches the Netherlands. When the Iraqi army arrests the Palestinian-Dutch Ibrahim I. in Iraq, one of his sisters seeks contact with a Shiite journalist who claims to have been present at the arrest. Ibrahim is the husband of the Dutch woman Laura H. who managed to flee from the Caliphate to the Netherlands. The journalist taunts and insults his sister – because to him, the family of an ISIS supporter is no less guilty than the perpetrator himself.

From this point of view, the ISIS-families in the Shahama camp have been collectively condemned for conspiracy to a crime, without any charges being brought or a lawyer of judge being involved. Human Rights Watch is protesting against this, and in the Laylan camp another human rights organization is standing up for the women there who were forced to marry men from ISIS. A court in Kirkuk is now attempting to determine just how guilty they really are. But if they are then given the official stamp of 'victim', where can they still go?

In their temporary home in Mosul, I start a conversation about this with my adopted family. Mays appears to be the most nuanced in her views, as due to her study of English and the books she reads, she likely has a more open view of the world. 'I think that it is wrong, because the families must really be proven guilty,' she says. 'Often the sons would join, and then were disowned by their families.' But her father Nasser and brother Mustafa believes it is justified to ban the ISIS families from the city. 'They deserve it, because they were accommodating to them, received money and accepted the situation. Only when the army arrived did they claim to have no relationship with Daesh, and that only their children had joined.'

Hanaa Edwar, from Al-Amal, is concerned about this collective conviction as guilty. 'You cannot punish people for something a family member has done,' she says with a sigh, while sitting on the couch with her dogs at home in Baghdad.

Edwar is known in Iraq for her critical and obstinate opinions, and on this subject, she is honest to her reputation too. Mentioning that the pamphlets in Mosul are no exception, as cities like Ramadi and Fallujah are not allowing ISIS families to return, she states: 'That is not healthy. We must convince people that it is still possible to live together. You will need a special program to achieve this, and you must then convince both sides to participate.'

She views the ISIS families as being 'a time bomb', due to their desperate situations. Factors are the drug abuse and prostitution in the Shahama camp, along with the fact that the children are still singing Daesh songs and the absence of any education for teenagers. 'They were under their influence for so long. We must find a way to neutralize this.'

She calls for the ISIS families to openly speak out against ISIS. 'Even if they are not responsible themselves, it might be a good thing if they were to officially offer their apologies.' Because they must return into society, she emphasizes. 'If you isolate them, then the result will be new hate and revenge. And a new Daesh.'

+++

ISIS has changed the lives of many women. The most extreme examples are the thousands of Yazidi women who were kidnapped and used as sex slaves. If they managed to escape, they usually discovered that their family was murdered, and they no longer had a house or home.

And the longer they remain in the clutches of ISIS, the bigger the change. Yazidi doctor and activist Mirza Dinnayi tells me, that the women who were freed after three years, are convinced that all of the Yazidis have been exterminated, and therefore there is not a single reason for them anymore to want to escape. Moreover, many women are now so psychologically damaged by the brutality they have been subjected to, that they will never be able to have a normal life without receiving professional help.

Many Yazidi women were forced to move with the fighters to Syria, and the same is true for many Iraqi wives. What happened to them after more cities were being liberated from ISIS, is anyone's guess. All ISIS-wives share the stigma that will control their remaining lives, including those who had a jihad al-nikah or were forced into a marriage.

Many women will go underground, or move to a place where no one knows them, leaving their family and friends behind. At least, if they have the financial means to do so. Perhaps they will survive by denying that they made a conscious choice and claiming that they are victims because their husbands were lured into ISIS. For many civilians, that is also how they prefer to see the situation.

A decision made by the highest Sunni authority in Iraq, the Diwan of Sunni Endowments, can be important to them. It accepted a fatwa (decision) made in February 2017, that women who were raped, of forced into having sex, must not be seen as 'sinners' but instead as victims and therefore may not be punished. The fatwa is very strict towards the perpetrators, who must be seen as infidels, and are to be executed if they claim they acted based upon the Islamic faith (such as with a jihad al-nikah).

Even though it remains to be seen how much influence this decision will have on the society (because how many suspects will indeed be punished?), it could eventually lead to more people accepting the fact that some women were really victims. A similar decision from 2014, taken by the spiritual leader of the Yazidis, directly resulted in Yazidi women who were able to escape from ISIS, being accepted back into the society and even permitted to (re) marry.

Also, the women who survived the occupation will bear the scars. Not only due to the occupation by ISIS, but also from the liberation. The violence that partly was directed towards them, resulted in many traumas. Like for the students in East-Mosul, who complain about having problems concentrating. Nora (22) recounts how ISIS evicted her and her family from their home, when the Iraqi army was getting closer. 'We had to walk to another occupied neighbourhood – in the dark to prevent the airplanes from seeing us. With only the clothes on our backs we lived with some family for forty-one days.' Fatma (19) was also forced to leave. 'We had to crawl through the holes they had made in the walls between our houses. Three days later, our house was liberated. We found bombs and military items there, because Daesh had used it.'

The memories are still fresh. While buzz of the low-flying helicopters, the dull sound of outgoing rocket fire and the noise of fighter jets that just dropped their load in West-Mosul do not seem to visibly affect them, the young women do become very emotional when telling their own stories. They tell me about an uncle, who was arrested when he tried to escape. About snipers in their neighbourhood. And Ayat's eyes fill with tears when she talks about her sister being killed by mortars ISIS fired into their neighbourhood during the battle with the army.

During the battle in West-Mosul even more civilians were endangered. They were killed as the result of the coalition bombing of ISIS fighters in the highly populated areas, or when ISIS shot and killed them without mercy while on the run.

All citizens of Mosul must once again learn to trust, or perhaps even learn to live with distrust. For many women the relationship with their husband has changed, perhaps also with his family, or hers. Some entered into a marriage that they now regret, because they were too young, or they hardly knew the man.

Women must reclaim their position in society, get back to work, regain respect. And at the same time, they must see to it that their children do not suffer any lasting damage, do not become radicalized or perhaps turn their backs on the Islamic faith all together. Like is happening in Iraqi Kurdistan, out of repulsion against ISIS' religious legacy. And from other Iraqi cities there are reports too, of young people rejecting the Islamic faith. Some join left-wing groups; communism is experiencing a small revival.

I hope that this dismissal of ISIS' standards leads to more freedom than before, and that the closed society in a city like Mosul will open more swiftly than normally would be expected, such as is evident with the Yazidis. But as yet, there are not sufficient signs that this hope will become reality.

What doesn't kill you makes you stronger. Is that also true for the women of Mosul? Perhaps for some, who have managed to hang onto their new-found authority to make decisions. And others, who have been forced to survive daily life without a husband.

Let me share the words of some students, who manage to see the positive effects in all of this. Nora says that she has learned to be more patient. Amina believes that she has grown through all the misery. And Muntar concludes: 'We were sitting in the middle of death, and we survived.'

And finally listen to my adopted family in Mosul, who lost everything to ISIS. They will rebuild their city, they promise me, and even name the term of two years to realize this. Nidal says: 'We must avenge Daesh by rebuilding.'

Marwa took hardly any time to replace a large number of the portraits of her family that were lost. Mays is working her way through the English novels I have brought her and with every new message, I am able to see the improvement in her language. These women refused to allow themselves to be defeated. Even though it is far too soon for them to admit, that what they have survived has indeed made them stronger.

EPILOGUE

The war against ISIS had not yet finished when I started on this book. Part of the truths about what the terror group did to those it had occupied or enslaved had yet to surface. I had finished my book about the fate of women under ISIS, *Slaves Wives and Brides*, but there still was so much left to write about that I had not been able to use for my journalistic reports.

In the beginning it had been hard to believe that the bloody stories about what ISIS did were all true. Since then, I found that most of what we heard was real. ISIS had run one of the most gruesome regimes of the past century in Iraq. And left Iraq even more traumatized than it already was.

That is why it was essential for me to look for even the smallest of shimmers of light in those dark times. That urge led to writing this book. Which of course still is not the end of the story.

Even after ISIS was finally (more or less) finished after the battle of Baghouz (in Syria, 2019), not all the kidnapped Yezidi women and children had been found. The search for them still goes on (mid 2023: still over 2500 missing).

Many of them got lost in the sprawling camps where ISIS families were locked up, Al Hol and Roj, after the final battle. It took some Yazidi women going underground in the camp to find some of them; others simply cannot imagine they will be able to have a life outside of it anymore.

Soon, the most radical women ran in Al Hol a sort of a small caliphate. To diffuse the dangerous situation there, dozens of foreign ISIS-women and their children were repatriated to their home countries, to be tried and punished. Syrian women were released to their tribal heads, and slowly, a few hundred at a time, Iraqi women also were repatriated to special rehabilitation camps in Iraq.

The family-camps in Iraq I mention in this book have been closed for years, and there now is still one camp left, Jeddah Camp outside Mosul. Here the Iraqi families go, but never to stay for more than a couple of months before they are forced to move out again. Many of them have nowhere to go, as I already predicted.

The scars that ISIS left are still visible, ten years after they started their rule with the capture of Raqqa Syria, and then Falluja and Mosul in Iraq. That city is still partly in ruins. The political situation has changed dramatically, with the Shiite forces that were set up to fight ISIS now an important military and economic power. Some speak of a new occupation; another result of ISIS' rule and the vacuum that it left.

And the women? Their situation has not changed so much since I wrote this book. The only major positive difference is the role young women in Mosul play in the cultural scene: in street art for instance, but also in the orchestras that blossom and in the debating cafes that have been able to capture the omnipresent feeling that freedom is now and needs to be celebrated. And the more modern habits displaced Arabs brought back from Kurdistan when returning home after liberation.

The big challenge is how the ISIS-women will be able to settle again. Will communities finally take them back, of which I have seen some promising examples. Or will the women be able to live on their own (as husbands and sons are in prison or dead) elsewhere? From what I've seen, that's only possible if they have some protection, for instance of good willing and strong neighbours.

As for the Yazidi women: many of the survivors are still living in IDP camps in the Kurdistan Region of Iraq. Some have been able to emigrate (mainly to Germany and Australia), some tried to reach Europe by paying smugglers, often dying in the seas in between. At the same time, many women who returned from the Caliphate were able to get married and restart life within their own communities. Some of the younger returnees who went to university surprisingly captured the best grades.

While many countries have now branded what ISIS did to the Yazidis as genocide, Iraq still has not. As ISIS members are tried in Europe for their part in the genocide, in their own country the genocide plays no rule in the trials. All ISIS-members are tried under the anti-terrorism laws.

In Iraq, Yazidis are still discriminated and even seen as unbelievers. At the same time, the children of Yazidi women by their ISIS captors are considered to be Muslim by Iraqi law – and refused by the Yazidi religious leadership. This prevents Yazidi women from fleeing, from Al-Hol but also from as far away as Palestine, for fear of losing their children when they return home.

The radical women in Al Hol will be a danger to the world for as long as they are not tried, just like the thousands of ISIS-men and boys still in prison in Syrian Kurdistan. In Al-Hol, the women are even forcing their sons that have not yet been moved out of the camp because of reaching puberty, to have sex with their young daughters, to secure the next generation of lion cubs. Which leads to at least sixty births a month among a population of only women and children.

ISIS is still active, underground in Syria and Iraq, being able to recruit locally, form cells and to conduct regular attacks. And always planning to liberate their comrades from the prisons, to keep their repeated promise of returning.

I dedicated this book to all the Nadia's and Fatima's who suffered under ISIS but were able to pick up their lives and came out stronger. For they are my heroines. That goes especially for Nadia Murad, who as a survivor was able to tell the world what happened to the Yazidis by writing a book and traveling around the world. She worked hard for her people, and still does, to overcome the disaster.

The ‘Fatimas’ who did the same for the Sunni and Shiite victims of ISIS, are far less well known. But I met them. None of this book, and its prequel *Slaves Wives and Brides*, would have been possible without the willingness of so many women to talk to me.

But also not, without the translators and fixers who helped me find them. I especially want to thank Lina here, one of the few women working in this trade that is so essential for journalistic reporting but is hardly mentioned as such. Lina was traumatized herself after fleeing from Syria to the Kurdistan Region of Iraq but preferred to show herself as no less tough than the boys. Those trips into the (moral) ruins of Mosul must have been harder for her than I realized at the time.

Many thanks are also due to Kifah, who helped me meet my adopted family in Mosul and many of the women I talked to. I miss her hospitality and lovely smile, as well as the many teas and the beautiful food that she would always offer.

Finally, it would be great to keep you updated about my activities as a writer. Sign up for my newsletter, and receive a short novella for free, by going to my website:

https://juditneurinkauthor.com/free-book-for-you/

Judit Neurink,
Athens, August 2023

If you enjoyed this book, you will also like

The Good Terrorist

A novel by Judit Neurink

Rose is shocked to hear her husband died in the Caliphate. His best friend becomes her lover. Together will they be able to find out the truth of what happened?

Is there love, hate and friendship inside the Caliphate, the Islamic state that the radical Muslim group ISIS created in Iraq and Syria? How do you survive in this land of terror, and is it possible even to get out of it alive?

The Good Terrorist is the story of Rose, who finds herself confronted with these questions when she is told her former husband was killed in the Caliphate. While she is still in denial, her new lover, who is also his best friend, decides to find out what really happened.

And the story of Dua and Amina, two Yezidi women captured by ISIS to become sex slaves, and the secret networks set up to get them out.

It is the story of a struggle for humanity under a rule of a group that imposed its brand of Islam on large parts of Iraq and Syria. A story of religion abused in their hands, violence, and slavery. But also of brave men and women standing up against it.

For more information and how to buy the book, go to the author's website: https://juditneurinkauthor.com/the-good-terrorist/

Violence Recycled
by Judit Neurink

A personal report of a journey spanning a decade in a country that has been moving from war to peace and back again.

Dutch journalist Judit Neurink arrived in Iraq in 2008 to set up a training center for journalists. She reported as a correspondent on the development in the Kurdistan Region of Iraq, the rise and fall of the Islamic terror group ISIS and the kidnapping and murder of thousands of Yazidis. She witnessed the division of Iraq based on ethnicity and religion and heard the ever louder call for a strong leader.

For her, it all led to a strong connection to the country. More so, when with the protests by young Iraqis against the corruption, lawlessness and violence, aroused new hope. At the same time, a vengeful ISIS reappeared as a threat – as the death of Abu Bakr al-Baghdadi had no effect.

Neurink came to help in rebuilding Iraq, but more and more had to report on tensions and violence. She could not remain immune from the suffering, and that eventually led to her leaving. In *Violence Recycled* she looks back at a tumultuous decade, and shows the reader the cultural diversity, deeply rooted conflicts and highs and lows of a country that she came to love, but for which a peaceful future seems an almost impossible dream.

For more information and how to buy the book, go to the author's website: https://juditneurinkauthor.com/violence-recycled/

ABOUT THE AUTHOR

Judit Neurink (1957) is a journalist and author from the Netherlands, a specialist on the Middle East who lived and worked in the Kurdistan Region of Iraq from 2008 to 2019, having witnessed both an economic boom, development and crisis, with the entry of the Islamic group ISIS in the region.

She set up a media center in Kurdistan to train journalists and teach politicians and police how to work with the media. After leaving the center, she worked for Dutch and Belgian newspapers, radio and TV, as well as international media.

She has written ten books, all of them connected to the Middle East, amongst them a novel about the Jews of Kurdistan. She now lives with her two Siamese cats in the Greek capital Athens and still reports on Iraq.

Printed in Great Britain
by Amazon